AUTUMN IN JAPAN

WOODBLOCK PRINTS BY HOKUSAI, HIROSHIGE AND OTHER ARTISTS

I0418850

AUTUMN IN JAPAN

WOODBLOCK PRINTS BY HOKUSAI, HIROSHIGE AND OTHER ARTISTS

Anne Sefrioui

PRESTEL

MUNICH · LONDON · NEW YORK

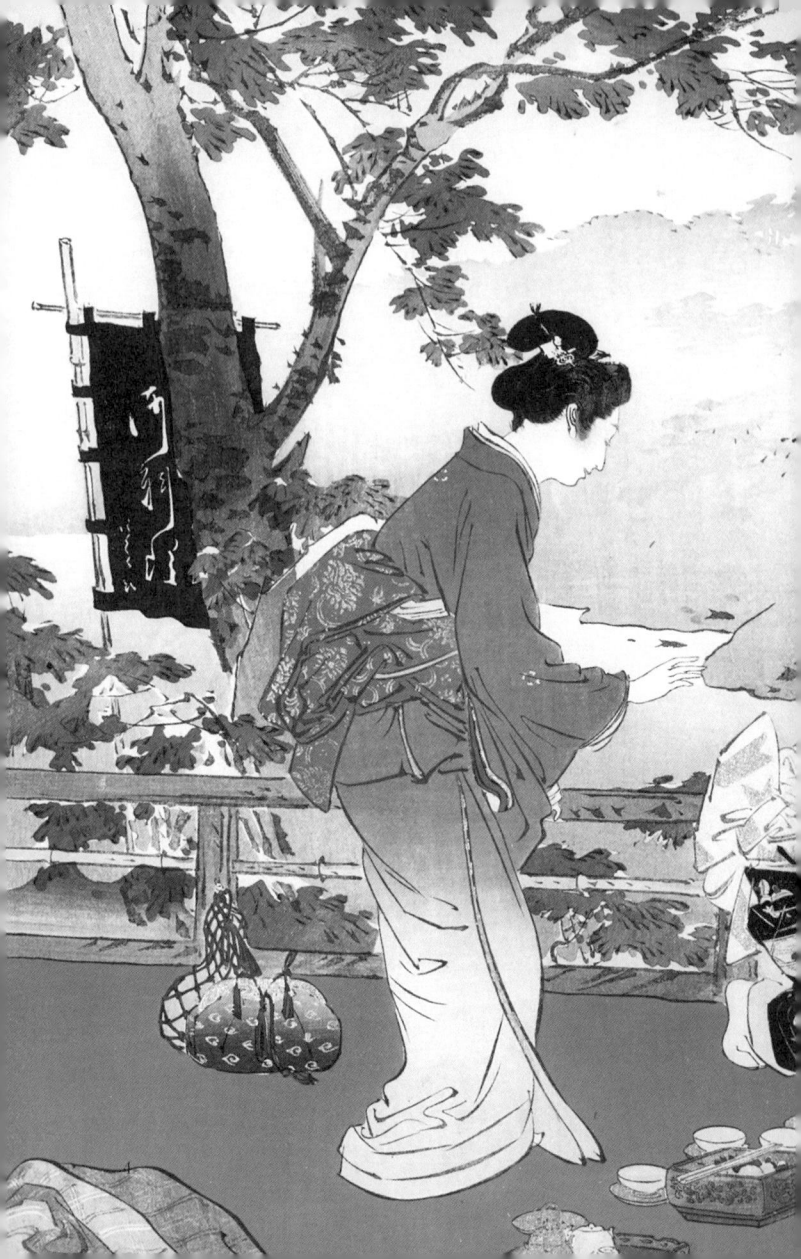

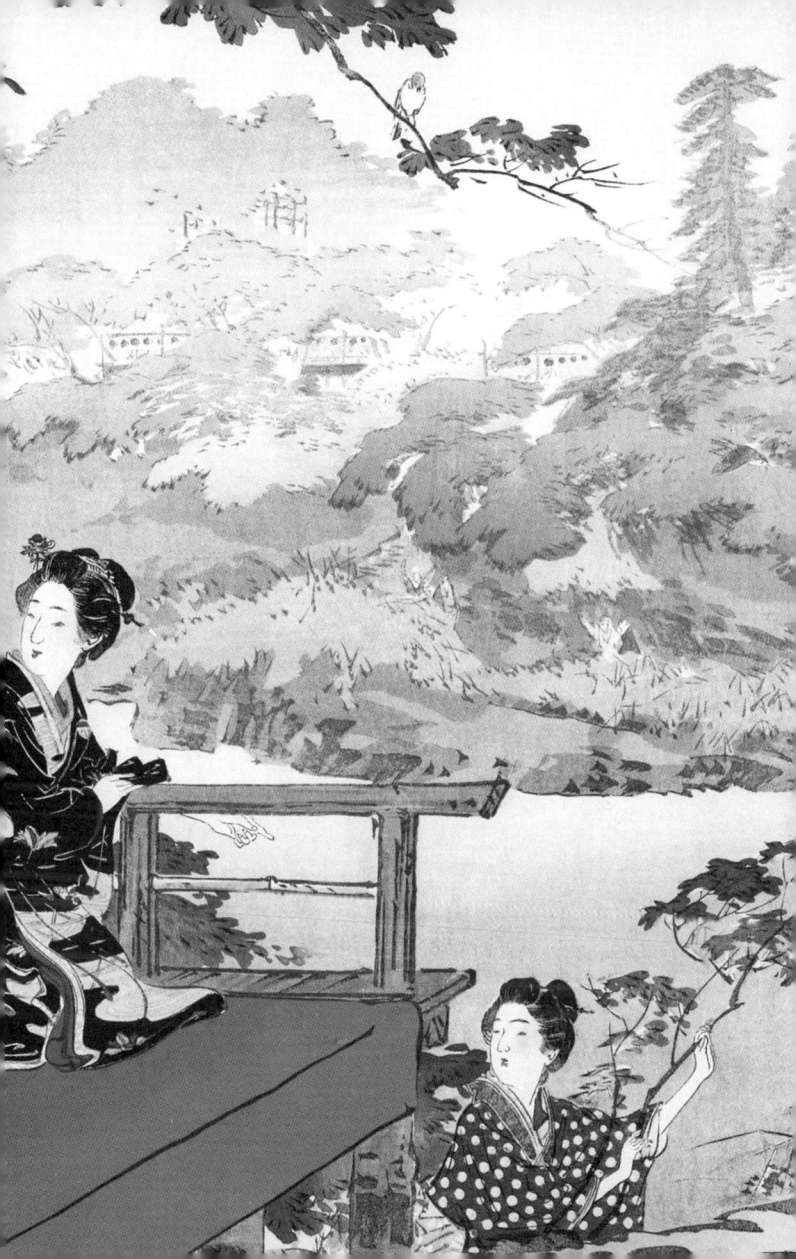

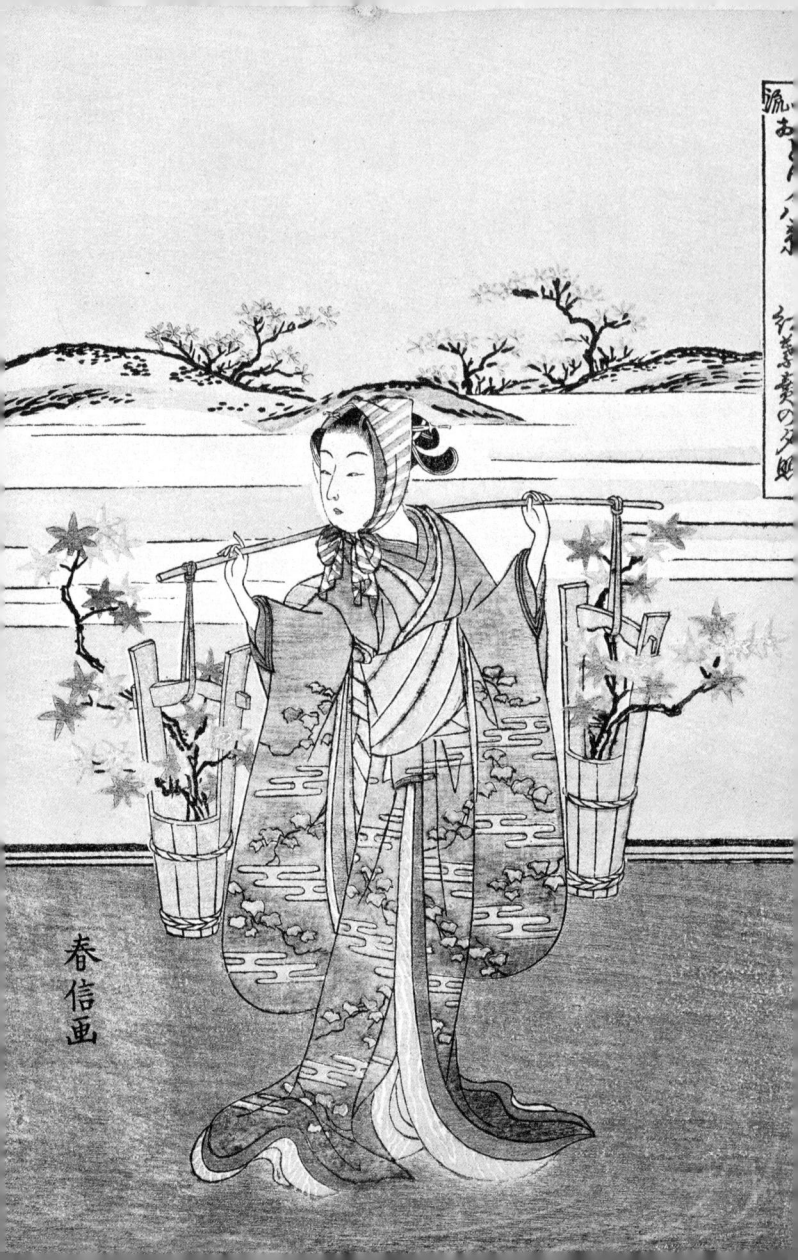

"When one goes to see the flowers in the springtime or contemplate the crimson foliage in autumn, should poetry not exist, none would know of colours and fragrances: where would one find the fundamental meaning of things?" This twelfth-century text illustrates the importance of poetry in Japanese culture and its essential role – making the world visible by expressing the feelings that it inspires within us. The Japanese people's intimate connection to nature and their attention to seasonal cycles explain why autumn, along with spring, is one of the most common themes in Japan's poetic tradition. As the concise form of the waka demands great sparsity of words, a visual or auditory detail is sometimes all that is needed to evoke this season. The onset of the first fresh breeze, for example, is one of the most frequently recurring motifs:

I cannot yet see it
Clearly with my eyes,
But the rustling of the wind
Made me realise
That autumn has arrived.

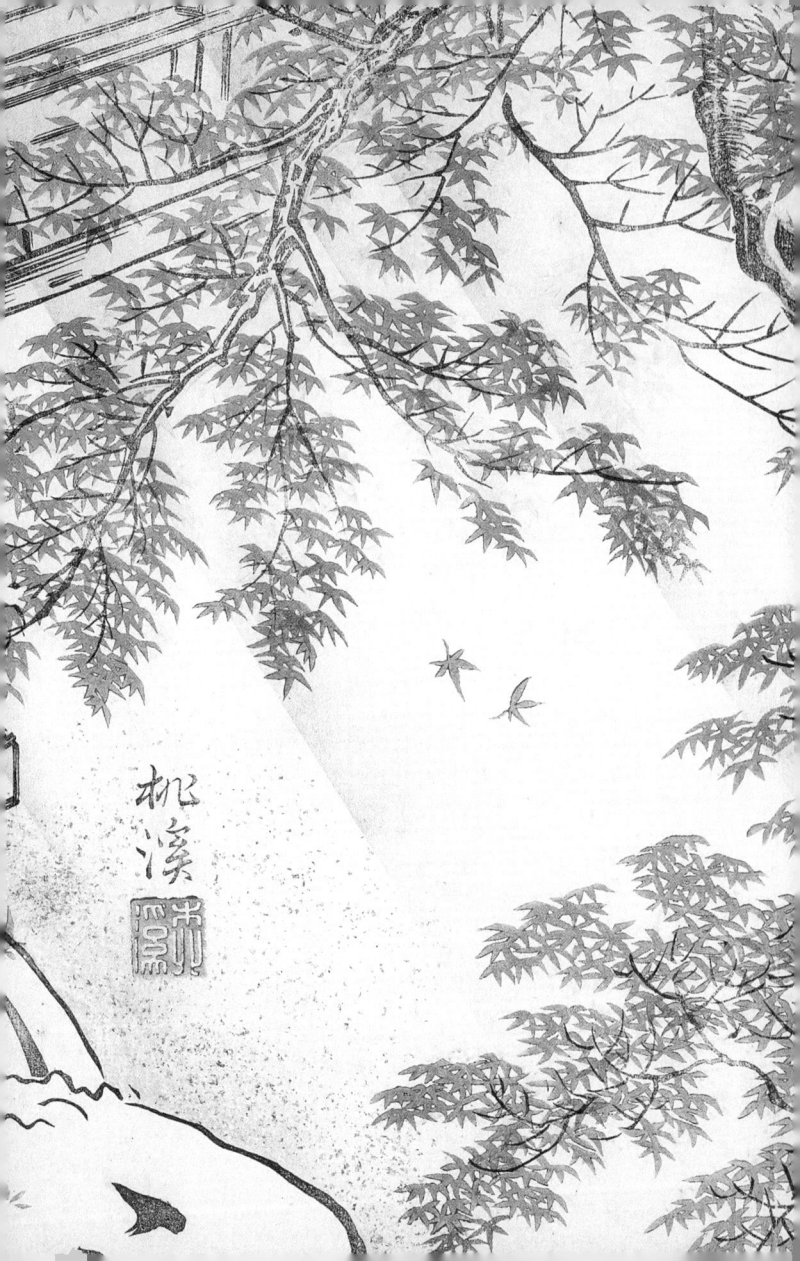

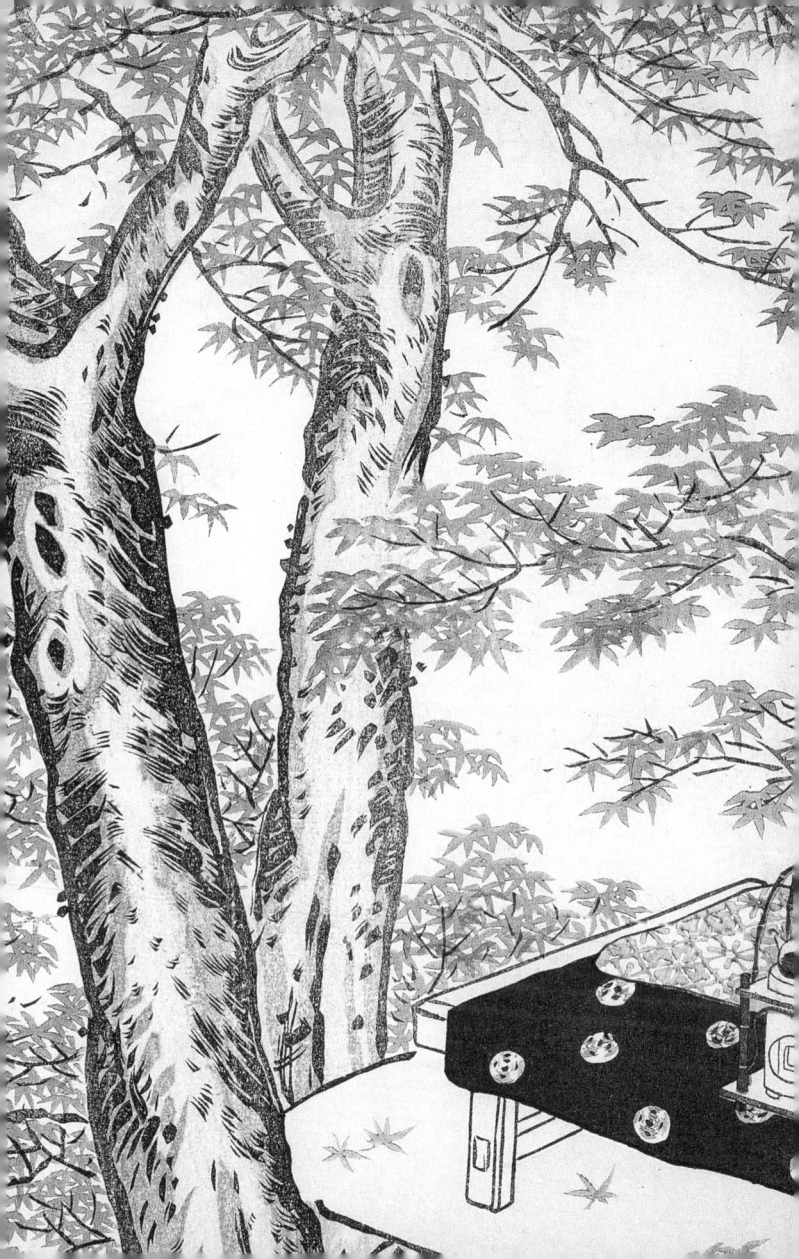

Poets were inspired by other signs of nature at this time of the year, such as the appearance of dew, the chirping of crickets which follows the song of cicadas, the bellowing of deer, or the flight of wild geese:

> *Carried by the autumn wind*
> *Comes a ship resounding with cries*
> *Towering high as hoisted sails:*
> *A flight of wild geese*
> *Crosses the strait of the heavens.*

Among the highlights of this time of year, two are of greater importance: the apparition of the autumn moon, which marks the beginning of the season, and a few weeks later, the contemplation of the maple trees. Both these events are cause for popular celebrations. The first, Tsukimi, is a festival that takes place on the fifteenth day of the eighth lunar month, according to the traditional Japanese calendar, i.e. towards the end of September. The celebration consists in the contemplation of the full moon on that night, as the weather is still gentle and the skies are particularly clear. Some gaze at the moon directly, their eyes raised, while others, adopting a more refined approach, rather admire its reflections in the water, as the famous poet Matsuo Bashō evokes in a haiku:

> *Harvest moon:*
> *Around the pond I wander*
> *And the night is gone*

Named the "harvest moon", the autumn moon is also associated with the cultivation of rice, which is harvested at this time of year. The Japanese people thank the nocturnal heavenly body for its generosity and for bringing them prosperity, and share the fruits of the earth with it. And so, when families and friends gather together, the contemplation of the moon features offerings that the guests will enjoy after observing the heavenly body: seasonal foods such as chestnuts and sweet potatoes – and above all, *mochi*, round treats made from rice dough, special to this festival.

The other major natural event marking autumn, the changing of the colour of the foliage, begins in September; dates vary according to each region's climate. While in spring, the blossoming of cherry trees begins in the south of the archipelago, then moves northwards week by week, maple leaves first turn crimson on Hokkaido, Japan's northernmost island, and the turning then descends southwards for the two following months. As with cherry blossoms, some places are particularly renowned for the beauty of the spectacle – certain mountains, in particular, but also large public parks and the gardens of the many temples and palaces. Many poems describe this phenomenon, such as the following:

> *By the wind storm's blast*
> *From Mimuro's mountain slopes*
> *Maples leaves are torn,*
> *Which turn Tatsuta River*
> *Into a rich brocade*

However, we all know that this beauty is fleeting, as the leaves turn a brilliant colour (*koyo*) just before they fall. It therefore comes as no surprise that many of the poems about autumn are imbued with a form of melancholy, especially as this spectacular visual display also heralds the approaching cold months of winter.

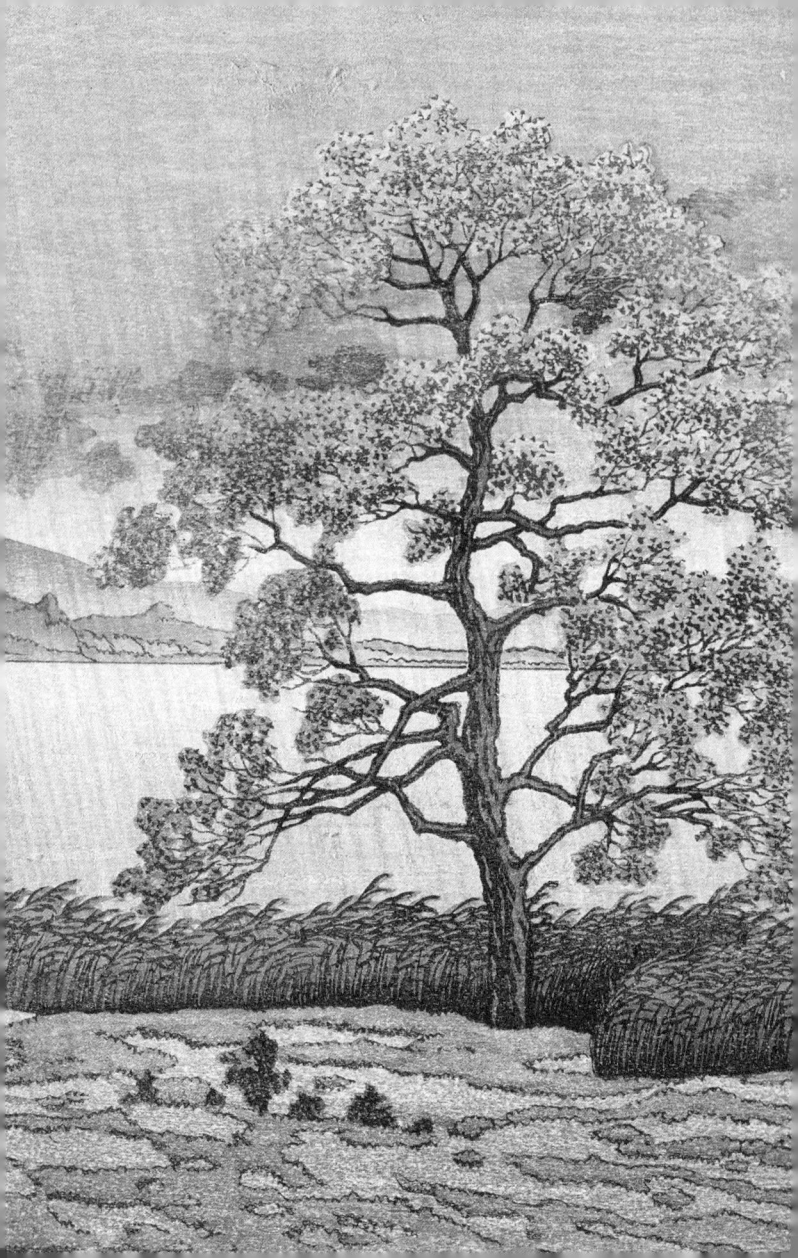

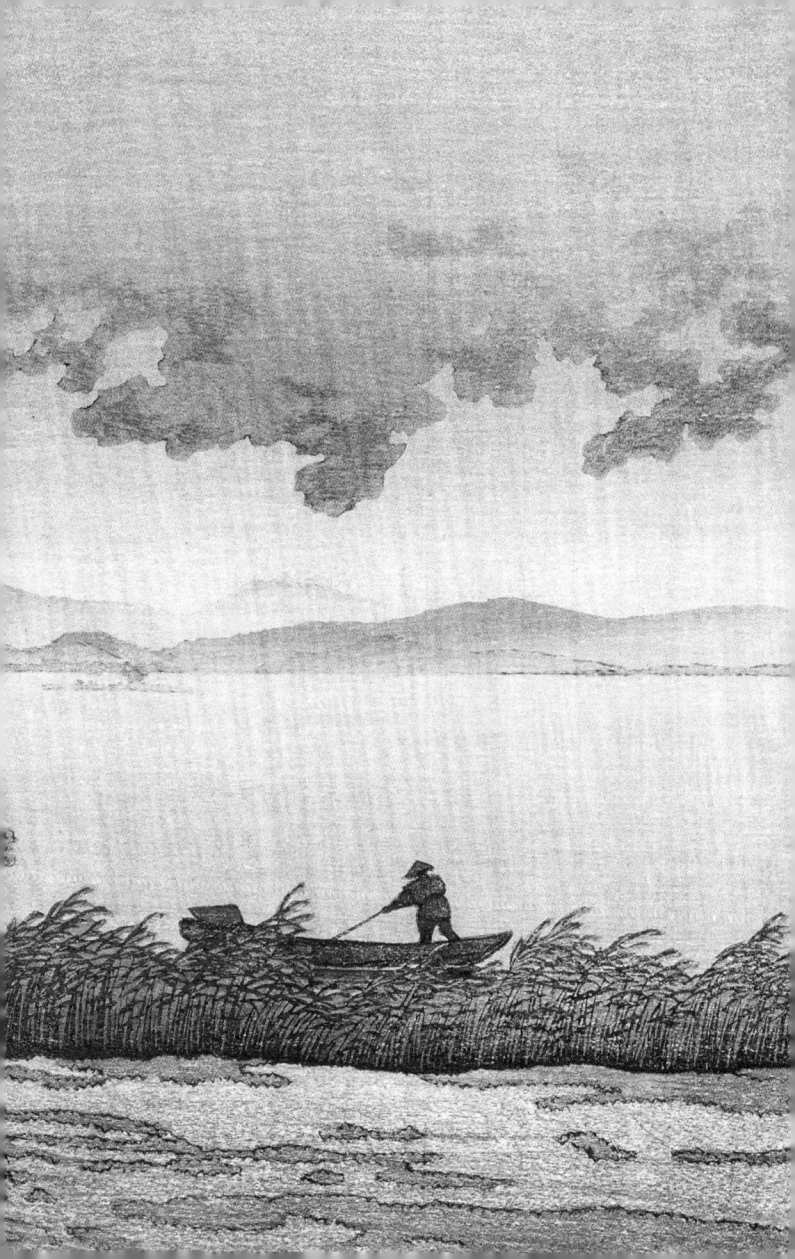

Though they have not yet fallen
Already I yearn for
The reddened leaves
I feel I now behold
The radiance of their final moments

The maple trees' ephemeral blaze, which disappears after their leaves have fallen to the ground, invites us all once again to meditate on the brevity of all things and on the frailty of human existence. It is on this notion of all things fleeting that, in the seventeenth century, the ukiyo-e movement was founded. Its meaning was described by the poet Asai Ryōi (1612–1691):

Living only for the moment, savouring the moon,
the snow, the cherry blossoms, and the maple leaves,
singing songs, drinking sake, and diverting oneself
just in floating, unconcerned by the prospect
of imminent poverty, buoyant and carefree,
like a gourd carried along with the river current:
this is what we call ukiyo.

In the 19th century, with the spread of colourful, inexpensive woodblock prints, representations of autumn and the season's enchanting atmosphere were met with huge popular success. As demonstrated by the works contained in this boxed set, which were produced between the 18th and 20th centuries, the theme was treated in every genre of ukiyo-e prints, starting with landscapes and famous views (*meisho*), of which Hiroshige was a renowned master (plates 2, 5, 6). One should note that maple trees are not always depicted in tones of orange or red, and some varieties have brown, ochre, pale yellow (pl. 12, 19, 62, 63, 64, 66) or even white foliage. As well as maple trees, oak trees are also taking on their autumn colour – a golden hue that is highly enjoyed by discerning onlookers.

At Saoyama
The oaks' yellow leaves
Are pale, yet
Autumn so deep
Has become!

In ukiyo-e prints, the genre depicting "flowers and birds" (*kachō-ga*), delicate shapes of plants are depicted with meticulous detail. Akin to other seasons, autumn is marked by the growth of certain species of plants, such as the patrinia, crowned with a large yellow flower (pl. 2, 43).

The autumn wind,
As it flows, brushes over
The patrinia:
My eyes cannot see it,
But by its fragrance, I know it!

Other autumn plants include "pampas grass", elegant grasses whose tall stems and brushes sway gently in the wind (pl. 2, 28, 43, 61), and buckwheat (*soba*), a cereal harvested in October and used to prepare noodles (pl. 33, 61).

However, the queen of autumn plants is unquestionably the chrysanthemum (*kiku*). Sometimes blooming as late as December (pl. 13, 14, 46, 47, 56), this flower is the symbol of longevity. Imported from China around the 7th century for its medicinal virtues, this flower became very popular, especially in the 19th century. Omnipresent in

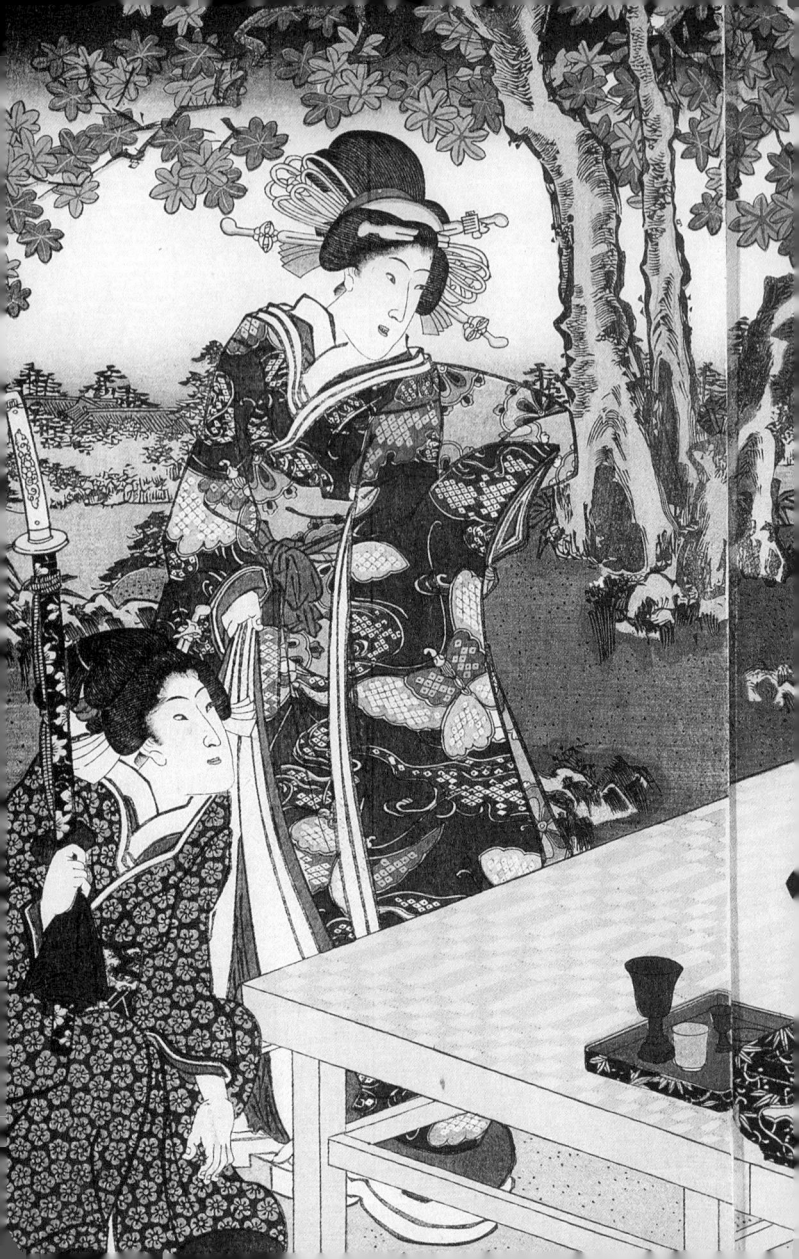

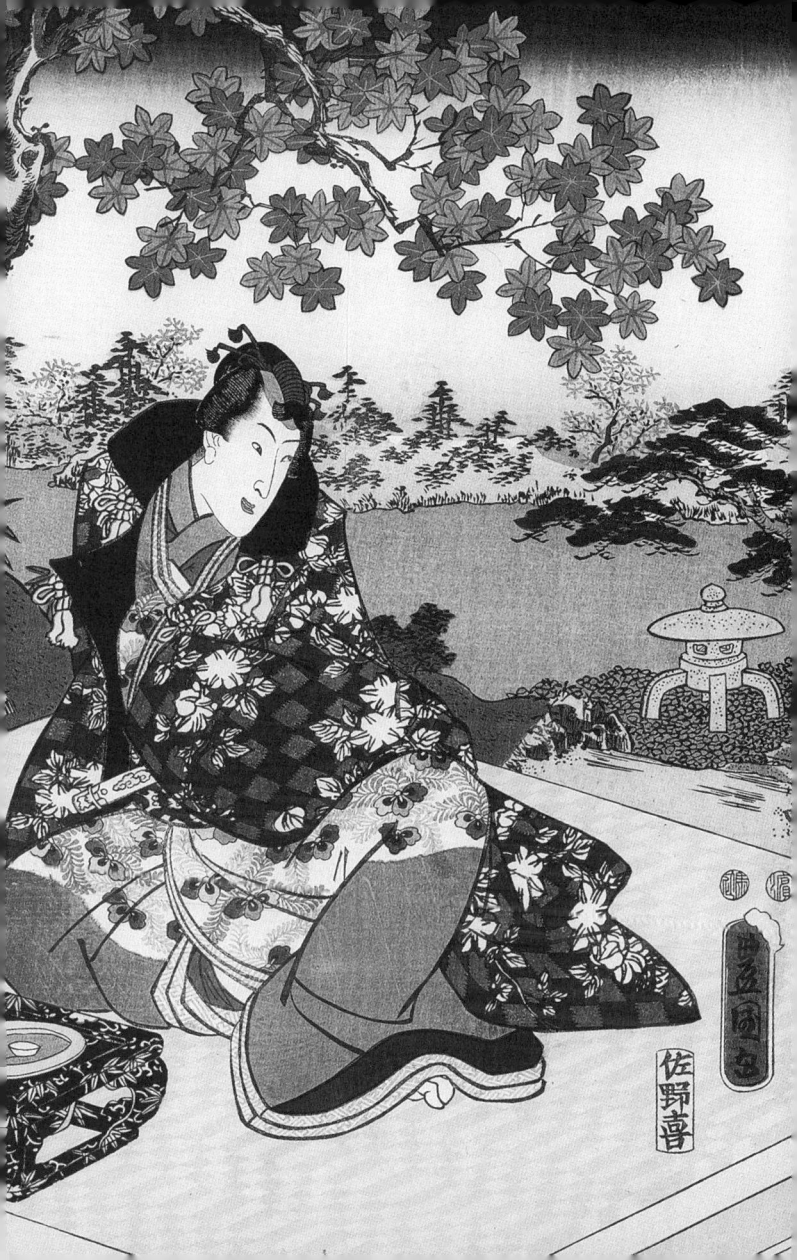

Japanese culture still today, it is the emblem of the imperial family, and appears on the passports of Japan's citizens. Craftsmen of the past already used this motif extensively, particularly on textiles: the chrysanthemum can indeed be found in interior decoration, on hangings and, above all, on many kimonos (pl. 19, 46), where it competes with another very popular motif: the maple leaf (pl. 37, 48, 52).

As *kachō-ga* also included representations of the animal world, woodblock prints also depicted insects and birds – tits or passerines (pl. 17, 22, 23, 29, 32, 33), and cranes, whose southward migration, beginning in September, heralds the end of summer (pl. 13, 14).

The iconography of autumn is clearly dominated by the contemplation of maple trees, *momijigari*. Over the centuries, this ritual, which remained long exclusive for the aristocracy (pl. 7, 16, 28, 35, 40), spread to all strata of society, from the bourgeoisie to simple peasantry. Whether alone or in a group, accompanied by family or friends, on a terrace or in a park, all of Japan's inhabitants are immersed in the admiration of the colours of the foliage: purple, carmine, vermilion, orange, all hues of red mingle to form a sumptuous bouquet, combined with the bluish tones of the conifers. Sometimes, a gust of wind accelerates the fall of the leaves (pl. 49, 50), which swirl in the air before falling down to the ground, forming, on rivers, an undulating carpet that can be observed from the riverbank (pl. 7).

Autumn is also the season of specific agricultural activities, beginning with the rice harvest at the end of September, evoked in prints by the alignment of the millstones (pl. 8, 10, 55), followed by drying, and then transplanting (pl. 57). Mushroom gathering is also a seasonal pleasure, sometimes indulged in by women and their children (pl. 37, 38). Only a few fortunate gatherers will unearth a *matsutake* – a highly prized mushroom, similar to a truffle, whose price makes it a luxury item. Lastly, another autumnal activity is the harvesting of maple seeds and leaves (pl. 58), which can be either cooked (pl. 24) or dried (pl. 60) for use in traditional medicines. Sometimes, some will simply cut a maple branch to make a bouquet (pl. 25, 54).

Prints featured here are not presented in strict chronological order, and definite differences in style can be observed. Their variety, however, based on themes recurring throughout decades, testifies to the popularity of the autumn theme and, more broadly, to the powerful bond between man and nature.

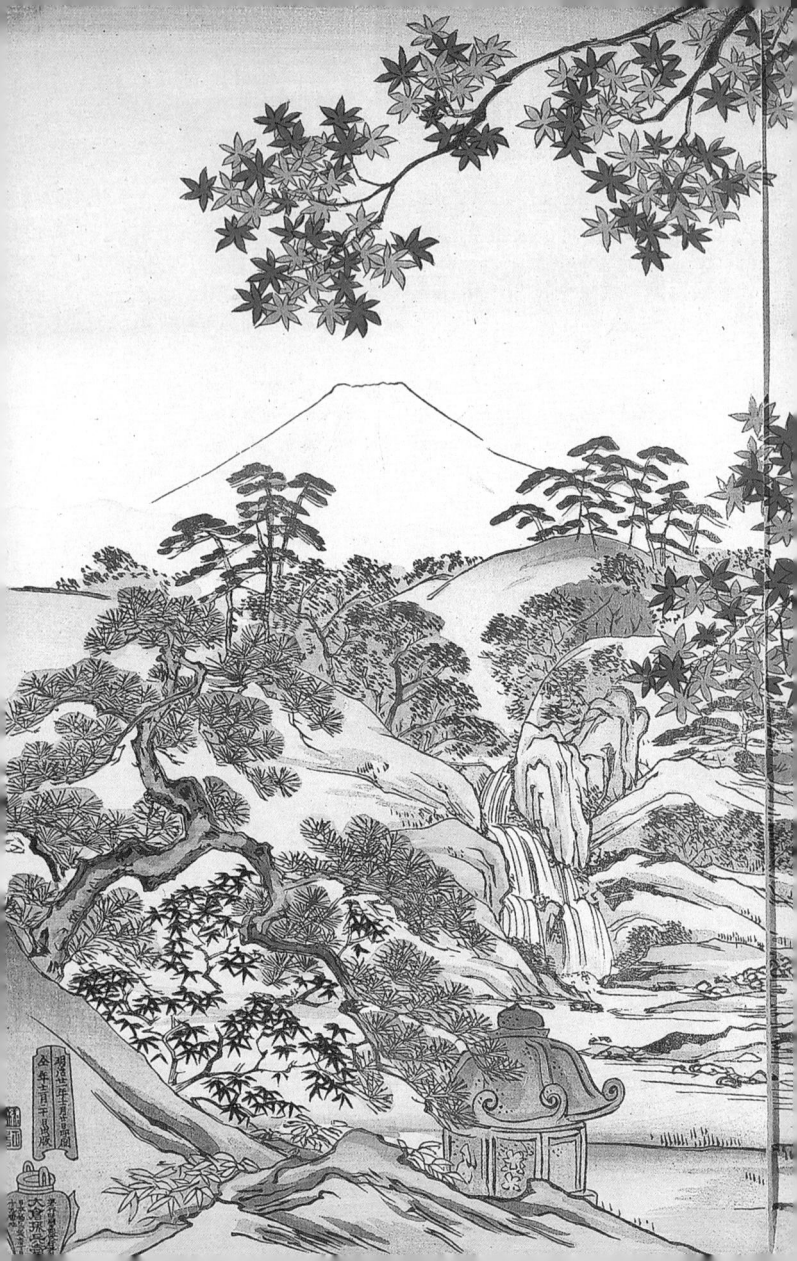

The great masters of printmaking presented in this book:

Ishikawa TOYONOBU (1711–1785)
Suzuki HARUNOBU (1724–1770)
Chōbunsai EISHI (1756–1829)
Niwa TŌKEI (1760–1822)
Katsushika HOKUSAI (1760–1849)
Katsukawa SHUNCHŌ (active 1780–1801)
Utagawa KUNISADA I (alias Utagawa Toyokuni III), (1786–1865)
Yoda CHIKKOKU (1790–1843)
Utagawa HIROSHIGE (1797–1858)
Utagawa KUNIYOSHI (1798–1861)
Nakamura CHOSHUN (active in the early 19th century)
Utagawa HIROSHIGE II (alias Shigenobu) (1826–1869)
Iijima KŌGA (1829–1900)
Utagawa KUNIAKI II (1835–1888)
Toyohara CHIKANOBU (1838–1912)
Taiso YOSHITOSHI (1839–1892)
Utagawa HIROSHIGE III (1843–1894)
Kono BAIREI (1844–1895)
Nakayama SŪGAKUDŌ (active 1850–1860)
Ogata GEKKŌ (1859–1920)
Suzuki KASON (1860–1919)
Keishu TAKEUCHI (1861–1942)
Mizuno TOSHIKATA (1866–1908)
Shosai IKKEI (active 1870–1874)
Tsuchiya KŌITSU (1870–1949)
Miyagawa SHUNTEI (1873–1914)
Ohara KOSON (1877–1945)
Kawase HASUI (1883–1957)
Kasamatsu SHIRŌ (1898–1991)
GYŌZAN (active in the late 19th century)
Kawai KENJI (1908–1996)
Toshi YOSHIDA (1911–1995)

Captions of previous pages

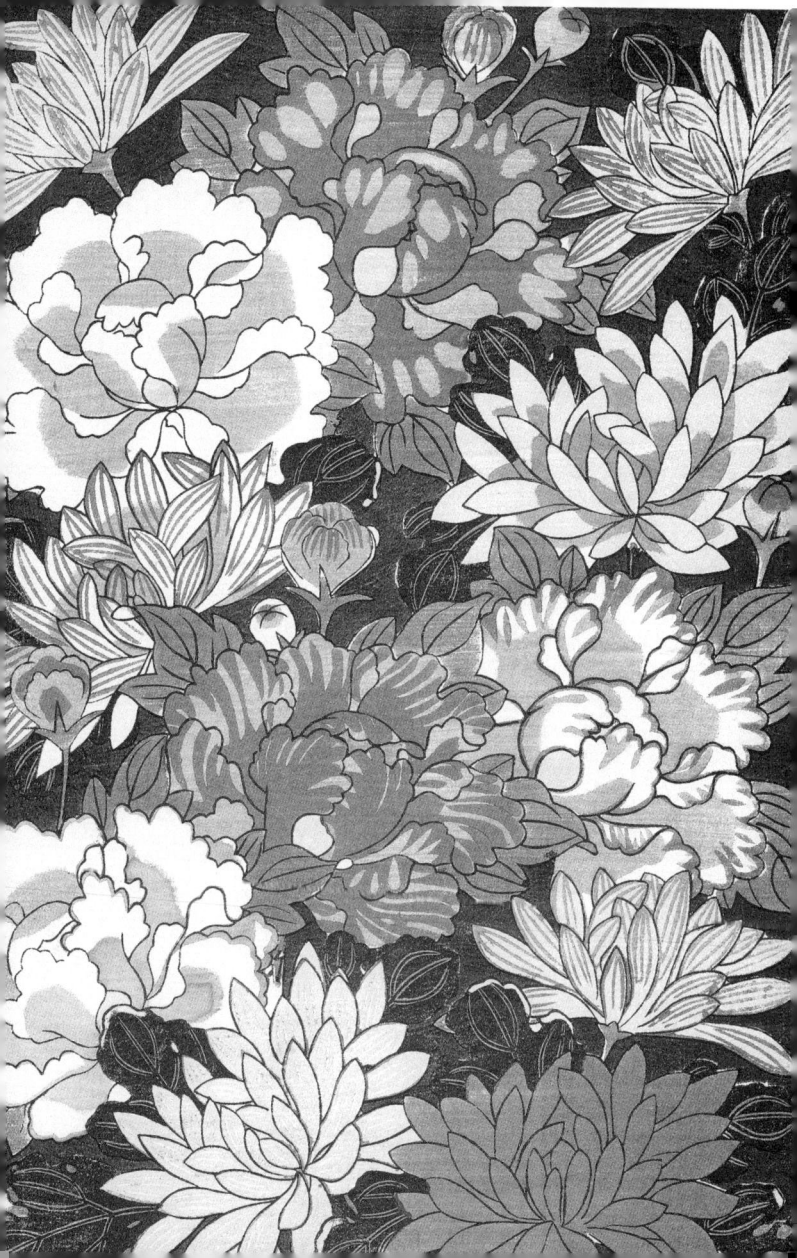

1| Katsushika Hokusai
Fresh Wind from the South
on a Clear Morning
(The Red Fuji), 1830–1832
From the series: *Thirty-six Views*
of Mount Fuji
25.4 × 37.8 cm

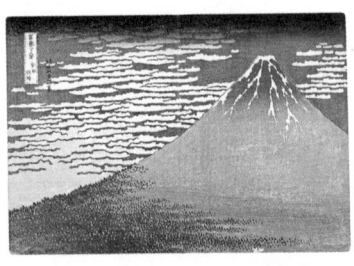

2| Utagawa Hiroshige
Otsuki Plain
in Kai Province, 1858
35.6 × 24.1 cm

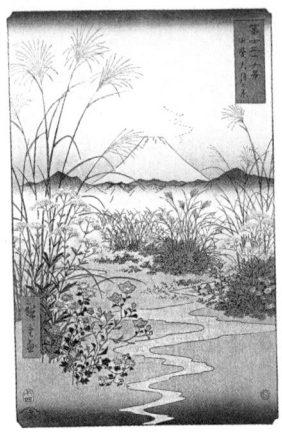

3| School of Maruyama–Shijō
Autumn Leaves, 1897
21.10 × 19 cm

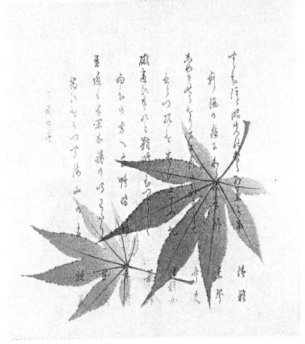

**4| Utagawa Hiroshige II
(alias Shigenobu)**
*Maple Leaves at Kaian-ji
Temple in Tokyo*, 1866
*From the series: Thirty-six
selected Flowers*
36 × 23.5 cm

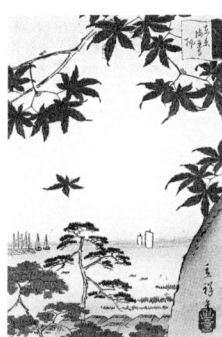

5| Utagawa Hiroshige
*Maple Leaves at Mama, the Tekona
Shrine and Tsugi Bridge*, 1857
From the series: *One Hundred
Famous Views of Edo*
36.1 × 24.4 cm

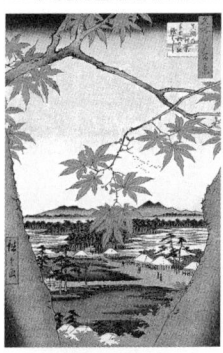

6| Utagawa Hiroshige
Inside the Akiba Shrine at Ukeji, 1857
From the series: *One Hundred
Famous Views of Edo*
35.3 × 23.1 cm

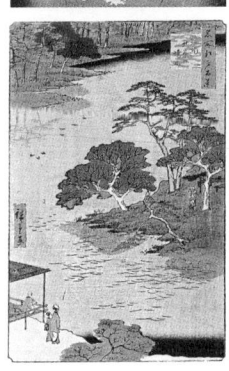

7| Utagawa Kuniyoshi
*Poet with Two Pages on
the Banks of the Tatsuta*, 1845
37.3 × 25.6 cm

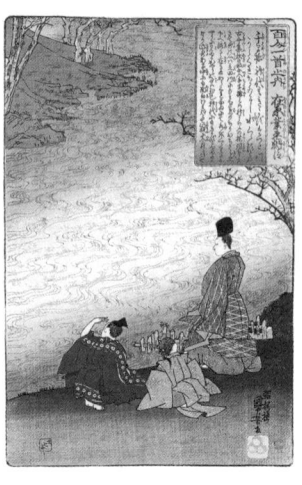

8| Katsushika Hokusai
Poem by Sarumaru Dayū, 1839
From the series: *One Hundred
Poems Explained by the Nurse*
25.4 × 36.5 cm

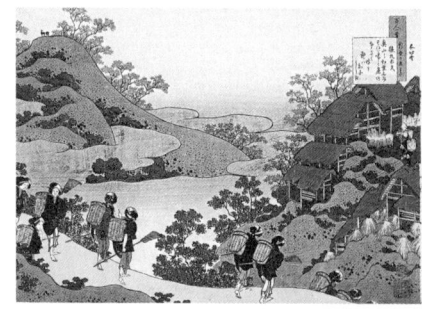

9| Unknown artist
*Illustration of the Maple Leaves
at the New Palace*, 1888
37.8 × 75.8 cm

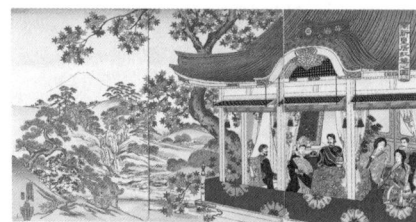

10| Katsushika Hokusai
Poem by Ariwara no Narihira, 1839
From the series: *One Hundred Poems
Explained by the Nurse*
25.7 × 38.1 cm

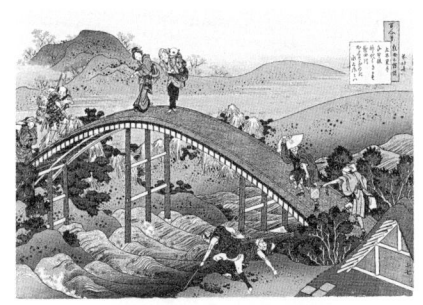

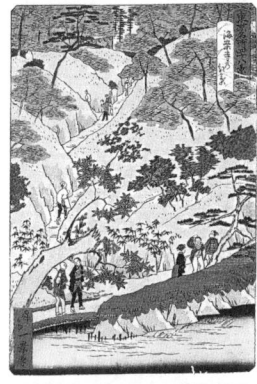

11| Shosai Ikkei
*Maple Trees at
Kaian-ji Temple*, 1871
From the series: *Forty-Eight
Famous Views of Tokyo*
36.1 × 25 cm

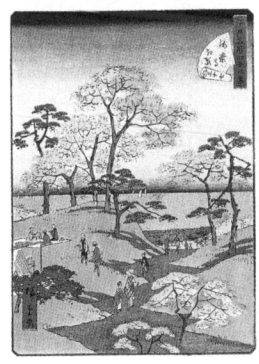

**12| Utagawa Hiroshige II
(alias Shigenobu)**
*Red Maple Leaves at
Kaian-ji Temple*, 1861
From the series: *Forty-eight Views
of Famous Places of Edo*
25.5 × 18.3 cm

13| Gyōzan
Red-crowned Crane,
Chrysanthemum, and
Autumn Grasses, 1878
From the series: *Plants and*
Trees, Flowers and Birds
38.5 × 25.2 cm

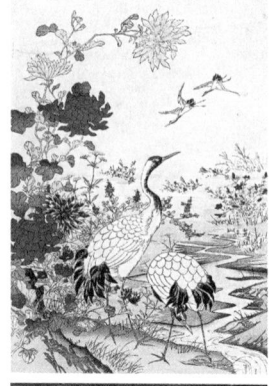

14| Utagawa Hiroshige
Crane and Autumn
Flowers, 1830s
21.9 × 16.6 cm

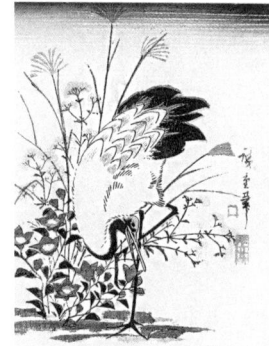

15| Katsushika Hokusai
Poem by Funya no Asayasu,
ca. 1835–1836
From the series: *One Hundred*
Poems Explained by the Nurse
24.8 × 36.5 cm

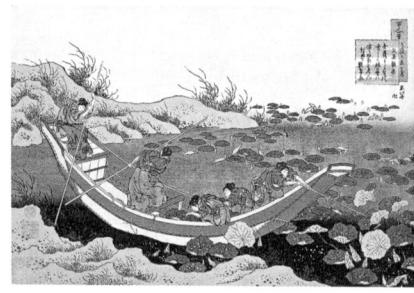

16| Katsushika Hokusai
Poem by Teishin Kō, 1835–1836
From the series: *One Hundred
Poems Explained by the Nurse*
25 × 37.2 cm

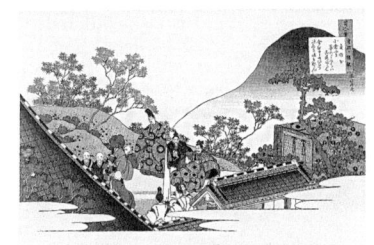

17| Nakayama Sugakudo
*Great tit on Branch of
Flowering Maple*, 1859
From the series: *Forty-eight
Hawks Drawn from Life*
36.7 × 25.1 cm

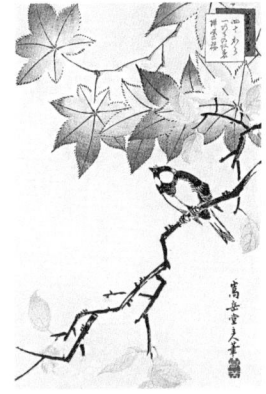

18| Mizuno Toshikata
*Noblewoman of the Tokugawa
Period*, 1891–1893
From the series:
Thirty-six Beauties
35.6 × 24.1 cm

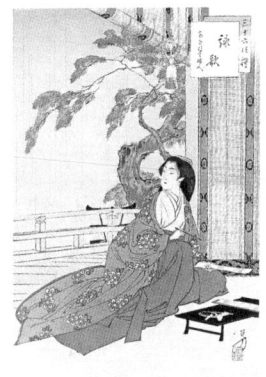

19| Mizuno Toshikata
*A Bright Tint of Foliage
in Autumn*, 1905–1906
From the series: *Mitsukoshi:
Brocades of the Capital*
30.2 × 35.6 cm

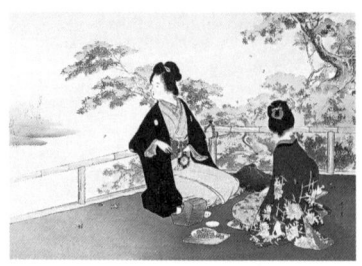

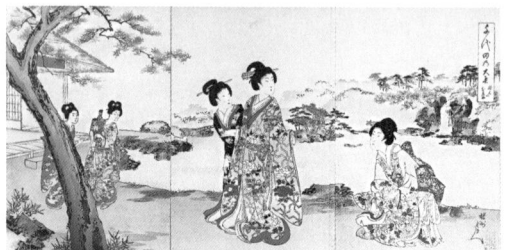

20| Toyohara Chikanobu
Chiyoda Castle, 1895
From the series: *Album of Women*
23.4 × 35.2 cm

21| Suzuki Harunobu
*Warming the Sake by
Maple Leaf Fire*, 1765
28 × 20 cm

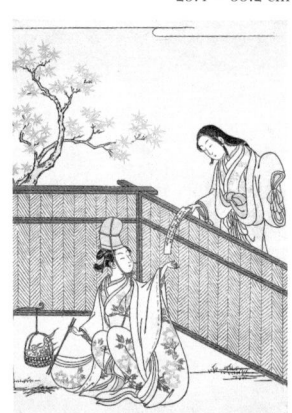

22| Kōno Bairei
Bird and Red Vine, 1893
21 × 26.9 cm

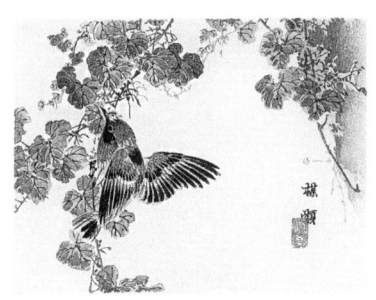

23| Utagawa Hiroshige
Japanese White-eyes on a
Maple Branch, 1854
33.2 × 10.8 cm

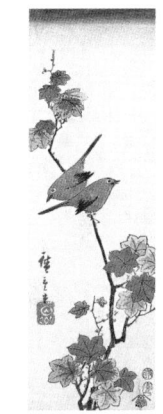

24| Suzuki Harunobu
Burning Maple Leaves to Heat
Sake on a Rainy Day, ca. 1766
28.7 × 21.6 cm

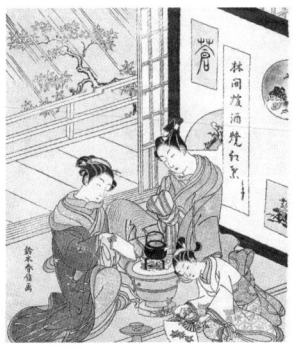

25| Ogata Gekkō
*Autumn Leaves at
Takinogawa*, 1896
35.9 × 71.8 cm

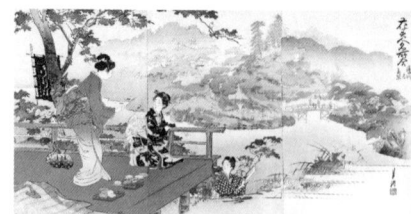

26| Yoda Chikkoku
Autumn Leaves,
first half of the 19th century
22 × 29.8 cm

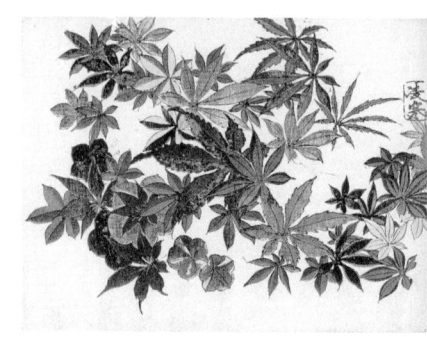

**27| Utagawa Hiroshige III
and Utagawa Kuniaki**
*Autumn Leaves at Kaian-ji
Temple, Shinagawa*, 1881
From the series: *Famous Views
of Civilised Tokyo*
36.3 × 25.2 cm

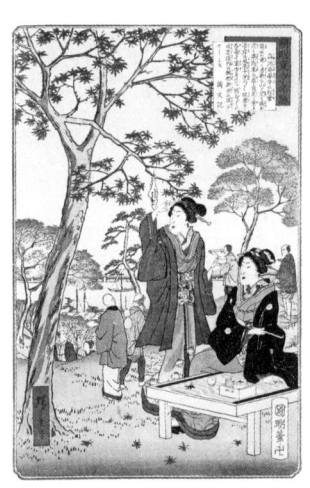

**28| Utagawa Kunisada I
(Toyokuni III)**
Moon, 1847–1852
From the series: *Snow, Moon
and Flowers, ca. 1847–1852*
36 × 73.5 cm

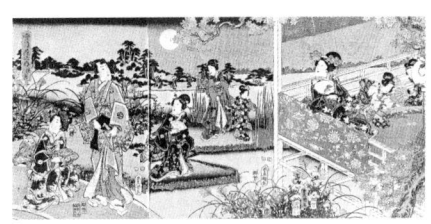

29| Ohara Koson
Great Tit on Paulownia Branch,
1925–1936
38.1 × 25.9 cm

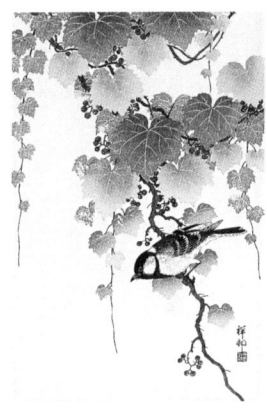

30| Miyagawa Shuntei
Beauties and Red Maple, 1897
From the series: *Refined
Customs and Manners*
38 × 25 cm

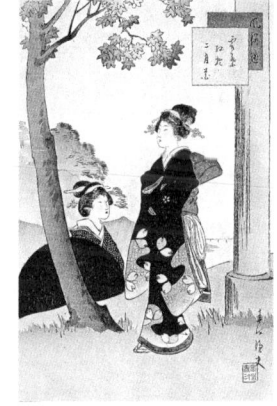

31| Chōbunsai Eishi
*The Yoshiwara Parade
in Autumn*, ca. 1793
38.8 × 74.3 cm

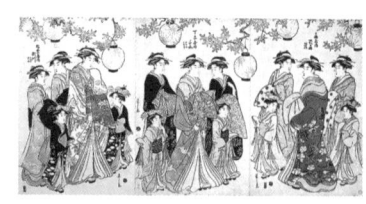

32| Iijima Kōga
Finch on Maple Branch
1890–1900
25.3 × 24.2 cm

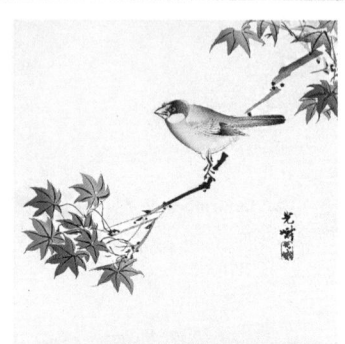

33| Unknown artist
*Autumn Flowers, Yellow
Bird and Insects*, 1875
35.7 × 23.6 cm

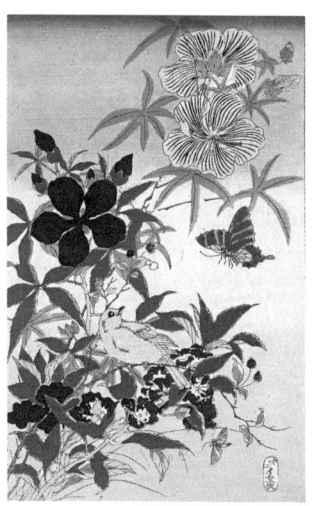

34| Toyohara Chikanobu
Moon Viewing Party, 1896
From the series:
Court Ladies of the Edo Castle
76 × 37.5 cm

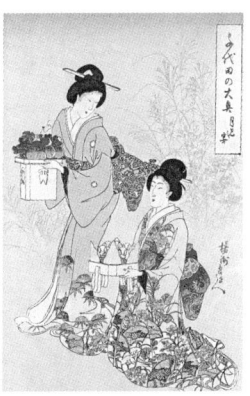

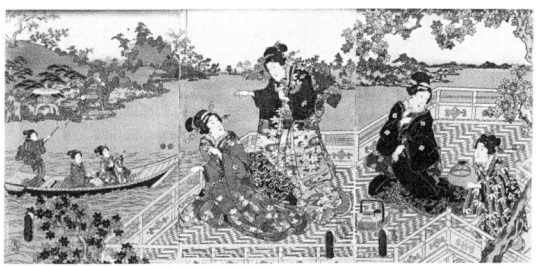

35| Utagawa Kunisada I (Toyokuni III)
Ladies on a Riverside Terrace in Autumn, 1851, 36.1 × 77.1 cm

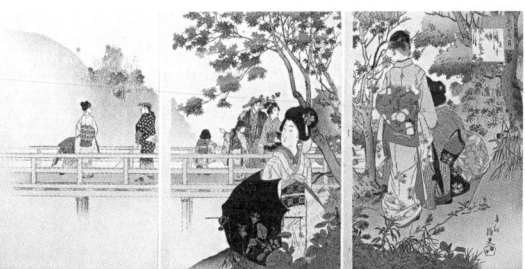

36| Miyagawa Shuntei
Beauties in the Twelve Months: October, 1898
37.6 × 71.7 cm

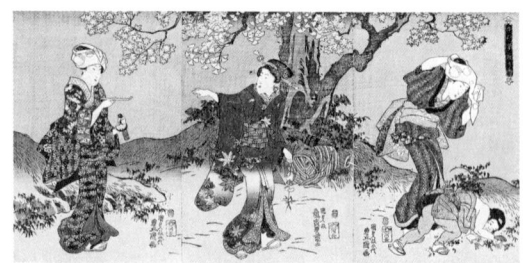

37| Utagawa Kunisada I (Toyokuni III)
*Gathering Mushrooms
in Mid-Autumn*, ca. 1844
36.4 × 74.3 cm

38| Niwa Tōkei
*Tea Stand for Viewing
Autumn Colors*, ca. 1810
38.1 × 49.8 cm

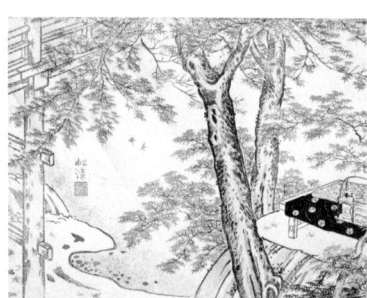

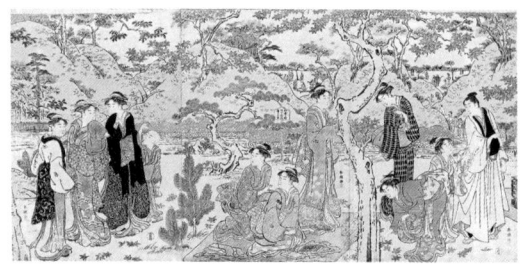

39| Katsukawa Shunchō
A Picnic Under the Autumn Maple Leaves,
ca. 1785–1789
37.3 × 76.4 cm

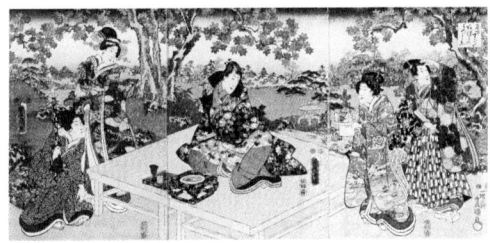

40| Utagawa Kunisada I (Toyokuni III)
Autumn Picnic Scene from Inaka Genji, 1847–1852
From the series: *Eastern Magic Lantern Slides of a Charming Figure*
36.4 × 75.9 cm

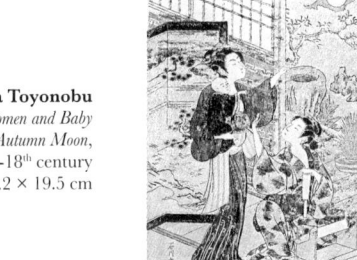

41| Ishikawa Toyonobu
*Women and Baby
Admiring Autumn Moon*,
mid-18th century
26.2 × 19.5 cm

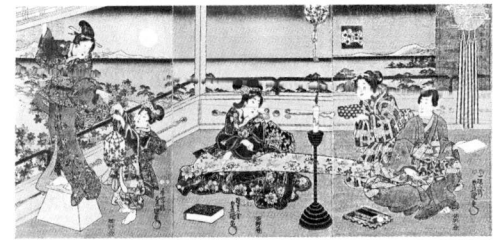

42| Utagawa Kunisada I (Toyokuni III)
Contemplating the Moon Scene from Inaka Genji, 1847–1852
From the series: *Eastern Magic Lantern Slides of a Charming Figure*
36.3 × 74.2 cm

43| Utagawa Hiroshige
Fan Print of Full Moon, Morning
Glories and Autumn Flowers, 1840
21.9 × 29.5 cm

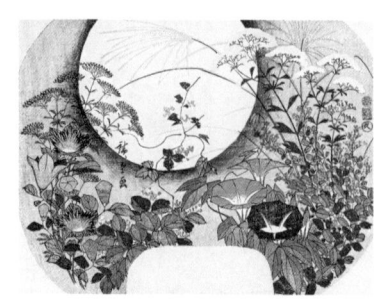

44| Keishu Takeuchi
Bijin in Flower Garden, 1903
29 × 23 cm

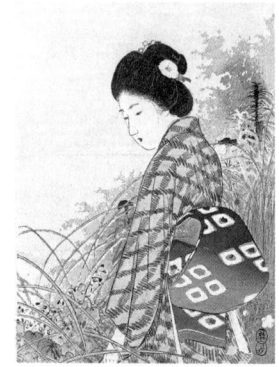

45| Suzuki Kason
Bijin and Umbrella, 1909
31 × 22 cm

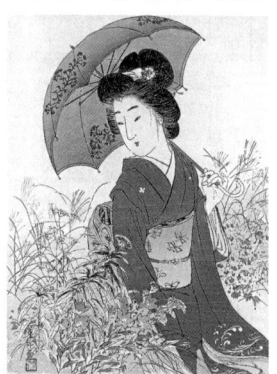

46| Suzuki Harunobu
*Young Woman by
a Riverbank*, 1766
28.6 × 21.7 cm

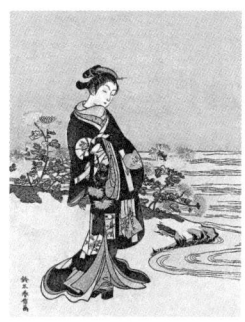

47| Unknown artist
*Decorative Paper with Design of Peonies
and Chrysanthemums*, 1866
38 × 25.7 cm

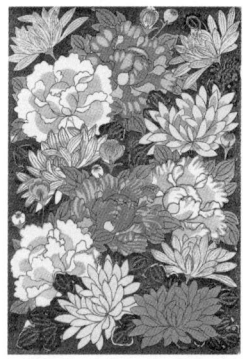

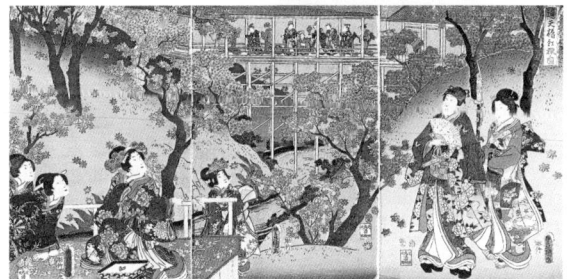

48| Utagawa Kunisada I (Toyokuni III)
Red Maple Leaves at the Tsūten Bridge, 1854
37.6 × 76.2 cm

49| Suzuki Harunobu
Maple-leaf dance, ca. 1765
28.6 × 21.7 cm

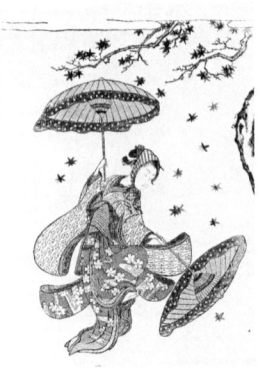

50| Taiso Yoshitoshi
Maple Leaf Gathering, ca. 1880
25.9 × 18.5 cm

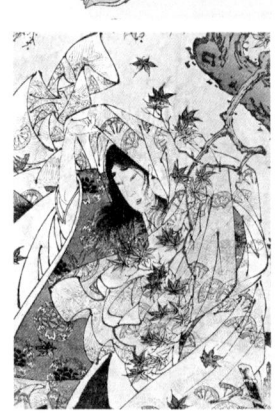

51| Nakamura Choshun
Birds and Autumn Foliage,
early 19th century
38.4 × 51 cm

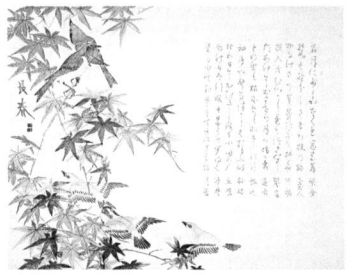

52| Suzuki Harunobu
*Sunset Glow of the
Maple-leaf Seller*, ca. 1769
From the series: *Eight Views of
Dances in the Modern Style*
22.3 × 16.5 cm

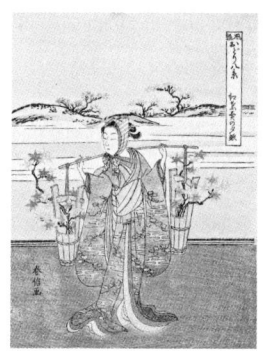

53| Suzuki Harunobu
*Two Women in the
Autumn Wind*, ca. 1767
27.3 × 20.3 cm

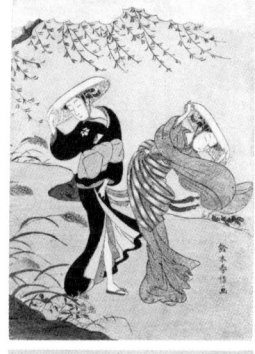

54| Suzuki Harunobu
*Young Woman and Man with Maple
Leaves*, ca. 1767–1768
26.8 × 20.9 cm

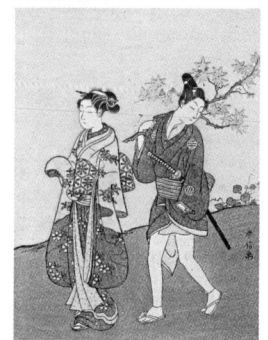

55| Katsushika Hokusai
Tenji Tenno (The Emperor Tenji),
First Poet, ca. 1830–1841
From the series: *One Hundred*
Poems Explained by the Nurse
26.2 × 37.7 cm

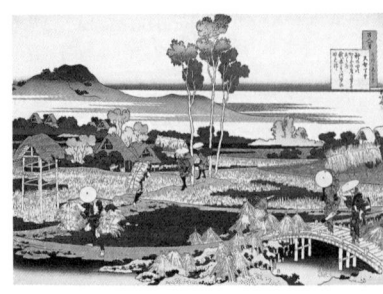

56| Tsuchiya Kōitsu
Chrysanthemums, first half
of the 20th century
26.4 × 29 cm

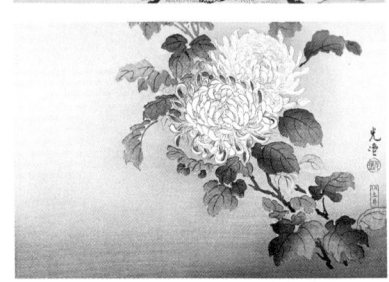

57| Utagawa Hiroshige
Hōki Province, Ōno, Distant View
of Mount Daisen, 1853
37.6 × 26 cm

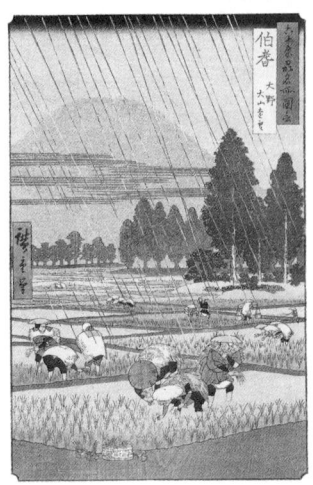

58| Katsukawa Shunchō
A Young Man, Two Young Women and a
Girl at a Picnic Party, ca. 1789
37 × 25.4 cm

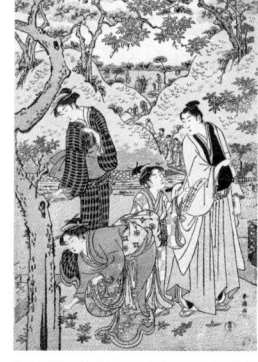

59| Katsukawa Shunchō
Bringing in a Rich Harvest in Autumn,
right-hand part of a triptych
1780s
38 × 25.2 cm

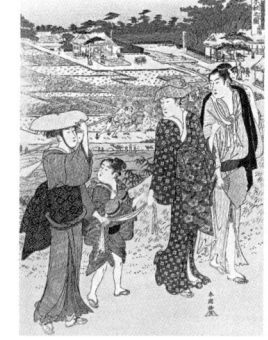

60| Kawase Hasui
Autumn in Koshiji, 1920
From the series: *Souvenirs of*
Travels, First Series
24.1 × 36.2 cm

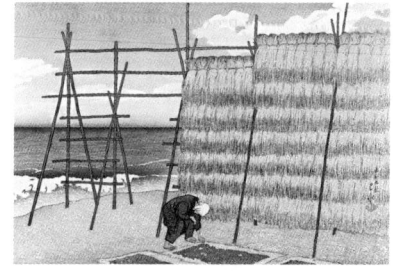

61| Kawase Hasui
Late autumn at Ichikawa, 1930
38.7 × 26.5 cm

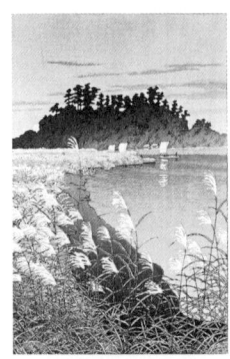

62| Kawai Kenji
Kiyomizu Temple in Kyoto, 1948
40 × 27 cm

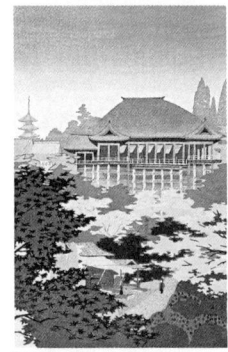

63| Kawase Hasui
Autumn at Oirase, 1933
38.7 × 26.1 cm

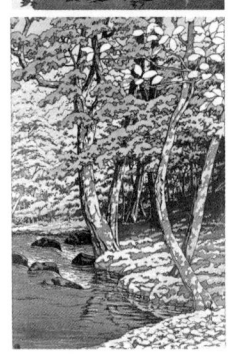

64| Toshi Yoshida
Autumn in Hakone Museum, 1954
40 × 27 cm

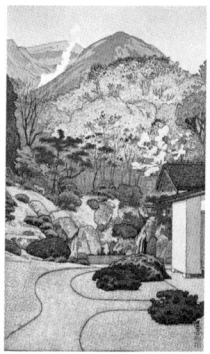

65| Kasamatsu Shirō
Kegon Waterfall at Nikko, 1952
36.2 × 23.9 cm

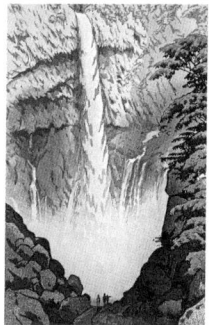

66| Kawase Hasui
Azuma Gorge (Azuma-kyō), 1947
36.4 × 26.9 cm

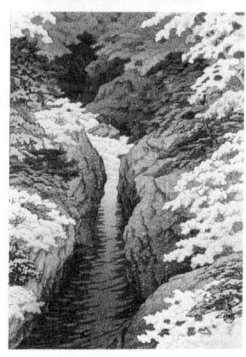

67| Kawase Hasui
Rain on a lakeside in Matsue, 1932
26.8 × 38.7 cm

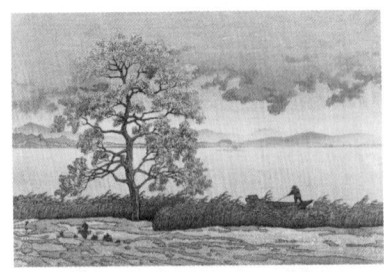

68| Kawase Hasui
The Garden in Autumn, 1920
Untitled series of views of the
Mitsubishi villa in Fukagawa
26 × 38.5 cm

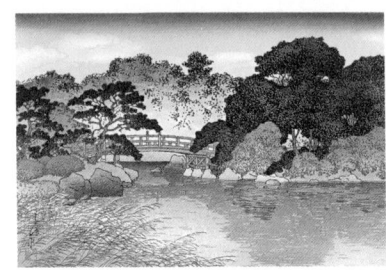

Opposite page
Suzuki Harunobu
Two Women in the Autumn Wind,
ca. 1767 (detail, pl. 53)

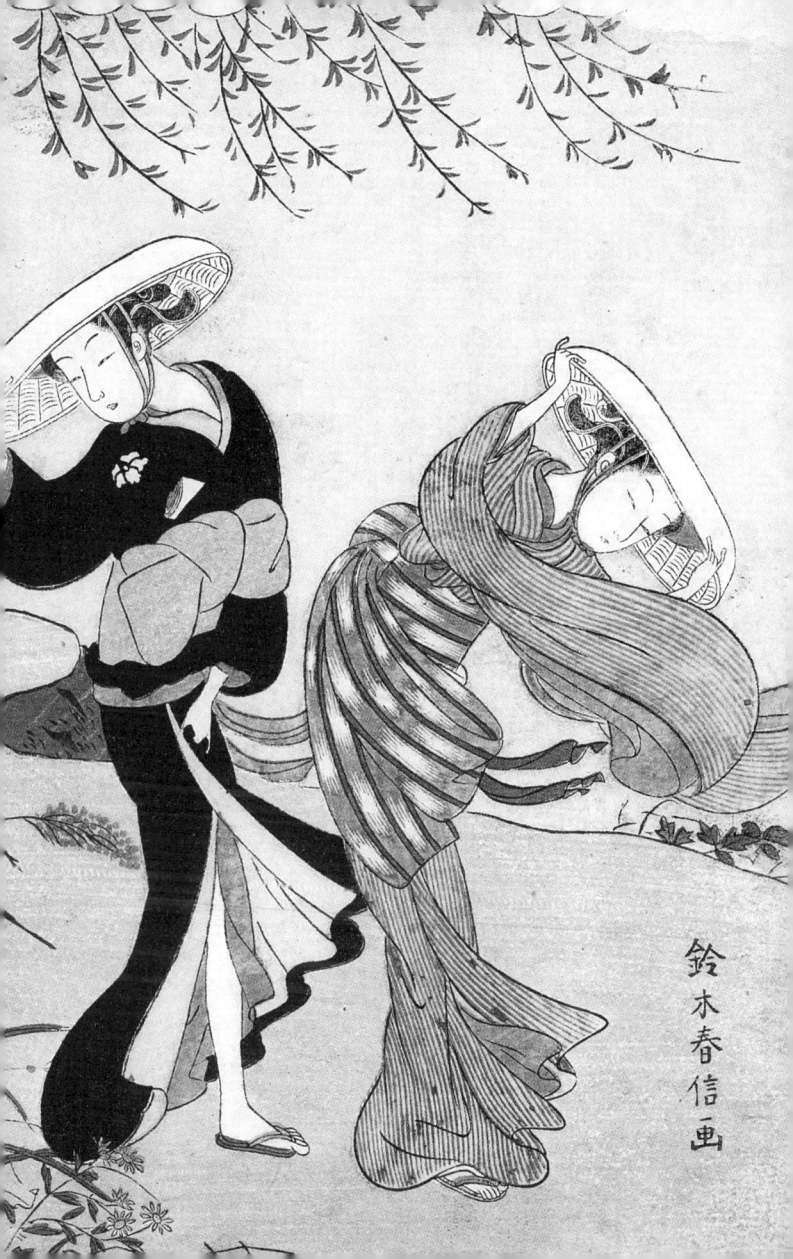

鈴木春信画

© Prestel Verlag. Munich · London · New York, 2025

Prestel Verlag
A member of Penguin Random House
Verlagsgruppe GmbH
Neumarkter Straße 28 · 81673 Munich

The publisher expressly reserves the right to exploit the copyrighted content of this work for the purposes of text and data mining in accordance with Section 44b of the German Copyright Act (UrhG), based on the European Digital Single Market Directive. Any unauthorised use is an infringement of copyright and is hereby prohibited.

A CIP catalogue record for this book is available from the British Library.

The French original edition was published by Edition Hazan as L'AUTOMNE

© Editions Hazan, 2023

Translation
David Rocher

Proofreading
John Stilwell

Production
Martina Effaga

Typesetting
Weiß-Freiburg GmbH, Grafik & Buchgestaltung

Lithographie
Hyphen-Group, Orio al Serio, Italie, Italy

Printing and binding
Toppan Leefung Printing

Printed in China

Penguin Random House Verlagsgruppe
FSC® N001967

ISBN 978-3-7913-9385-8

www.prestel.com

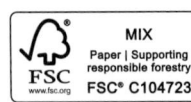